DASHER
LEARNS TO
SHARE

Dave Martellaro

Dedication

I dedicate this book to my very good friend, wife, and significant other, Bonnie. Bonnie, provided me the motivation and ideas to continue the life and adventures of Dasher. Her almost daily interactions and walks with Loki provide further adventures for me to write about for children to enjoy and parents to read to. Bonnie joined me with Angel, her Chihuahua, who also brings excitement and fun with Loki.

This book brings forward the difficulty and training that Loki required to accept Angel. Much like a baby coming into the family with an older child already there.

About the Author

I was born in South Bend, Indiana, where I spent my childhood and much of my teenage years. I attended Northern Illinois University and have been in IT for what seems like all my life. I have always enjoyed telling stories, whether from books or making them up for children to engage their imaginations. My intention in writing these stories about Dasher's exploits was to capture and highlight important life lessons to help children deal with everyday life. Also, as a parent, I enjoyed sitting with my children and reading to them, as I hope this will also draw parents into reading to their children. When not working or writing, I enjoy watching college football and movies with Dashers' inspiration, my dog Loki.

Dasher lived with his dad, Ben, and with the family of Mother, Father, Suzi and Jimmy. Dasher had a very happy and fun life with the family and with Ben. Suzi and Jimmy, who were responsible for keeping Dasher bathed, groomed, fed, and walked, spent hours playing with Dasher and teaching him tricks and commands. Dasher enjoyed his time with Suzi and Jimmy and looked forward to it everyday.   Father spent most of his time with Ben while Mother made sure both dogs were well taken care of and their needs met.

One day Father was visited by another man. Ben told Dasher that the man's name was Daniel. Ben said that Daniel was a very close friend of Father. Today Daniel brought another dog with him and Father recognized him as Ranger, a dog Ben had known for a long time and spent time playing with and talking to. The man Daniel left, and Ranger stayed with Father. Ben thought that Ranger may be staying a while since this had happened previous times, before Dasher was born. Ben had also spent time over at Ranger's house.

4

After Daniel had left both Suzi and Jimmy began playing with Ranger. Mother asked Suzi and Jimmy to give Ranger a dog treat and to take Ranger for a walk. When Dasher saw this, he ran over wanting dog treat and a walk, also. Mother said to Dasher, "Not now Dasher, maybe later". Dasher sat down and watched Suzi and Jimmy leave the house with Ranger. He felt sad he could not go too.

Later that afternoon Father started playing with Ranger and with Ranger's toys. Father accidentally picked up some of Dasher's toys and allowed Ranger to play with them. This made Dasher very angry and he tried to take his toys back. This made Ranger worried and frightened and he quickly moved away . When Father saw this he scolded Dasher. This made Dasher very unhappy and he ran off to his bed. He wondered why everyone was suddenly liking Ranger more than him.

When Dasher's father, Ben, saw what had happened and saw Dasher in his bed unhappy, he knew he better talk to his son. Ben wanted to know why Dasher was acting like he was. It wasn't like Dasher to be unfriendly with other dogs. He was friendly with Jock the Scottish terrier next door, and always played with other dogs at the park

"Son, what is wrong? Why are you unhappy?", asked Ben.   Dasher explained that since Ranger had come over, the family was ignoring him, playing with Ranger and not with him, letting him play with his toys, giving Ranger his dog treats, and then Father scolding him. "Dasher, Ranger is a guest, just visiting for a few days. Everyone is trying to make him feel welcomed and one of the ways is to share what we have with him.   This will make him feel welcomed.   When I go and stay with Ranger, his family does the same with me.", Ben explained to Dasher.

"I have an idea", Ben said to Dasher. He suggested that Dasher go to Mother, who knew when Dasher wanted a treat, to go ask for one. Ben led Dasher to the kitchen where Mother was, and Ben waited for Dasher to get a dog treat. Mother noticed Dasher sitting patiently and waiting for a treat. Mother said "What a good Dasher", and opened up the dog treat jar and gave one to Dasher.

14

After Mother gave Dasher a dog treat, Ben said to Dasher, "Now take the treat to the other room and place it in front of Ranger". Dasher was confused, he put the dog treat on the floor and asked his father why? Ben told him that by doing that, he was showing Ranger he was welcomed and you were sharing your things with him. Ben continued saying, "This will make you two friends and will let the family know that you are welcoming him here. Also, when you go to Ranger's home, he will share with you".

Dasher realized that his father was right and he picked up the dog treat and went into the room where Ranger was. Father, Suzi, and Jimmy were also there. Ben followed him in with Mother behind him. Dasher walked up to Ranger, who was a little afraid because of what had happened before. Dasher placed the dog treat in front of Ranger and stepped back and sat. Ranger picked up the dog treat and started eating it. The family and Ben waited to see what would happen next.

Ranger finished the dog treat and then leaned over and licked Dasher's nose. Ranger then rolled a toy in Dasher's direction. The family yelled out with cheers and clapping while Ben smiled. Suddenly Dasher felt happy while Suzi and Jimmy patted and praised him. Ben walked up to Dasher and asked him, "Do you feel better now?"." Yes ", Dasher said.

Later that night, when everyone was going to bed, Dasher took Ranger to Dasher's bed and offered it to him. Feeling happy that Ranger laid down in his bed, Dasher saw Ben call him over to share his. Dasher snuggled up to his father and fell asleep feeling happy on how the day had turned out and the fun Ben, Ranger, and he would have the next day.

The end

www.ingramcontent.com/pod-product-compliance
Lightning Source LLC
Chambersburg PA
CBHW041153150726
48006CB00015B/1965